EDITOR IN CHIEF

STEFANIE FRIESE

PHOTOGRAPHY BY

FLAVIA RENZ

WORDS BY

HANNI HEINRICH

COVER DESIGN BY

NAROSKA DESIGN, BERLIN

PUBLISHED BY

FRIESE MEDIA GMBH, 2018

1ST EDITION - AUGUST 2018
PRINTED AND BOUND IN BERLIN, GERMANY
ON FSC CERTIFIED UNCOATED PAPER

ISBN   978-3-9819822-2-0

SAY HELLO

GENERAL ENQUIRIES: hello@travelcolours.de

DISTRIBUTION: distribution@travelcolours.de

OR COME VISIT US ONLINE

www.travelcolours.de

PALMA

CITY GUIDE *for* DESIGN LOVERS

The Travel Colours City Guides are for design-loving travellers who like to explore the trendiest places in each city, for travellers who see themselves as trendsetters. Each City Guide features a curated selection of the best places to "sleep, eat, drink, shop and explore", all of which have been personally tried and tested.

Edition ONE

STEFANIE FRIESE

It has to be nice and a bit different. The desire for lifestyle and design is always guaranteed. As the founder of Travel Colours, Stefanie travels the world in search of the most beautiful places to sleep, eat, drink, shop and explore.

FLAVIA RENZ

Being based in Berlin, Flavia loves to keep herself surrounded by all that is beautiful and yummy. Camera in hands, you usually find her standing on any furniture available, just to get that picture framed perfectly.

HANNI HEINRICH

As a writer, Hanni is inspired by people, human behaviour and beaches. Her favourite body lotion is sun blocker factor 50. Born in Merseburg, Germany, she is currently based in Cape Town.

LOVE LETTER

Excellent restaurants, vibrant Tapas Bars, cozy beach and city cafés, glamorous boutique hotels, rich in history, and splendid beaches with crystal clear water - Palma has the benefits of both a traditional, yet modern and vibrant city and a striking seafront location. An explosion of new trendy places during the last years changed the so-called 'pearl of the Mediterranean' considerably and makes it more beautiful today than ever. Yet, despite the modernity, the Mediterranean flair can still be felt in every corner.

This Palma Guide will show you a curated selection of our favorite places to "sleep, eat, drink, shop and explore". From cozy coffeeshops, where young, trendy people sip their lattes, local Tapas Bars and internationally acclaimed gourmet restaurants, to some of the most beautiful Finca retreats, this guide will lead you away from the tourist hubs to some of Palma's hidden local gems.

Stefanie Friese

EDITOR IN CHIEF

SLEEP

PORTIXOL

EXCLUSIVE BOUTIQUE HOTEL

This chic boutique hotel occupies an exclusive position in the Portixol harbour, directly overlooking the glittering Mediterranean sea, with the entrance just a few steps away from the sea. With its stylish white façade, blue shutters and an overall nautical theme, Portixol gives the feel of a luxury yacht. A funky fun fish tank in the entrance emphasizes the Mediterranean lifestyle. The contemporary and spacious lobby, bar and lounge are bright white and airy with big comfortable sofas and vibrant cushions. At the popular restaurant you can enjoy a beautiful terrace overlooking the sea, whether you are here for a relaxing breakfast, lunch or a romantic dinner.

Carrer Sirena, 27, 07006 Palma
www.portixol.com

ES PRINCEP

SMALL LUXURY HOTEL

At this hotel, unique luxury meets the charm of Mallorca. Es Princep is situated in a quiet corner of the old town overlooking the Cathedral and offers magnificent panoramic views of Palma Bay. The spacious rooftop terrace with an infinity pool, a luxurious spa and two restaurants makes this place the ultimate urban getaway. The hotel is chic and modern with plenty of natural light, and good ventilation. There are 68 elegant and tastefully decorated rooms liveried in neutral shades. Contemporary art, dark wood furniture and flooring, and taupe-hued sofas are featured across all rooms. The hotel restaurant Balaroja serves gourmet Majorcan and Mediterranean cuisine in a quiet ambience and offers exposed excavations from a medieval tannery for the would-be archaeologists.

Carrer de Bala Roja, 1, 07001 Palma
www.esprincep.com

NAKAR HOTEL

TECHNOPHILE'S LUXURY PARADISE

The Nakar Hotel is a modern design hotel on Avenida Jaime III - one of the busiest and most emblematic shopping streets on the edge of the historic old town. This design hotel is an airy, bright and contemporary space aimed at fulfilling the needs of the modern traveller. Every Sunday, brunch is served on the rooftop while a DJ entertains with loungey tunes. Spread over five floors, the 57 sound-proofed, oak-floored rooms are spacious and bright with earth-hued textiles, multiple plug and USB sockets, Smart TV, mood lighting and sensors to detect human presence. Nakar also offers 10 interconnecting rooms for families and complimentary cots as well as sofa beds in all the suites.

Av. de Jaume III, 21, 07012 Palma
www.nakarhotel.com

SANT FRANCESC HOTEL SINGULAR

19TH-CENTURY MANSION

Today, this former 19th-century mansion is a boutique five-star hotel. Situated in Palma's old part of town, it is close to the city's leading attractions, including galleries, cafés and shops. The Sant Francesc Basilica with its delightful cloisters, the Palma Cathedral, the Almudaina Palace and the Arab baths are only a five-minute walk away. The hotel has a warm, relaxed and pleasant ambience. Visitors feel at home here, rather than like being guests. Many original features of this hotel have been retained, including frescoes and moldings. Large windows and arched doors still preserve the authentic feel of the building. A highlight of St Francesc is the roof terrace which should not be missed, whether for a refreshing bath in the pool or to enjoy the splendid views over Palma.

Plaça de Sant Francesc, 5, 07001 Palma
www.hotelsantfrancesc.com

SUMMUM PRIME BOUTIQUE HOTEL

CONTEMPORARY LUXURY HOTEL

Formerly a magnificent 16th-century palace, this artistically refurbished five-star boutique hotel offers a comfortable stay while keeping its delightful historic character. Situated in the atmospheric Gothic Quarter, it is close to major sights and the shops. This hotel is elegant and combines modern furniture with white walls. Original stone floors give the hotel a comfortable and contemporary feel. Each of the 18 rooms of the Summum Prime Boutique Hotel offers guests a personalized experience: unique aromas, colours that vary thanks to the brightness and an exquisite decoration which have been designed to provide maximum comfort. The building, which is a symbol of elegance, also boasts the latest technology, bringing modernity and style to the luxurious Palacio.

Carrer de la Concepció, 26, 07012 Palma
www.hotelsummum.com

HOTEL CORT

DESIGN CITY HOTEL

Hotel Cort is a small design hotel located in the centre of Palma de Mallorca. From here, all the historical sites in Palma de Mallorca are only a few minutes walk away. All 16 rooms, each unique, have been designed by Lázaro Rosa-Violán. Hotel Cort's rooms and suites are designed to create a feeling of well-being and warmth. A soothing palette of cool white, blue and ultramarine colours represent the Mediterranean Sea. The hotel's Mallorquin restaurant on Plaça Cort provides an excellent locale for guests to mingle with locals. This central plaza is home to Palma's Baroque-era town hall and a centuries-old olive tree that donates cooling shade and acts as a natural meeting point for locals.

Plaça de Cort, 11, 07001 Palma
www.hotelcort.com

HOTEL MAMÁ

CONTEMPORARY LUXURY HOTEL

The décor and interior of Hotel Mamá is an art work of renowned Parisian designer Jacques Grange. Close to Palma's top attractions such as the Cathedral, Almudaina Palace and Es Baluard modern art museum, Hotel Mamá offers an eclectic style with jazzy twist coated with floral patterns. Statement art is combined with exquisite textiles in a bold palette of hues. The tiles on the floor are certainly an eye catcher. Indeed, the extravagant monochrome marble and vibrant tile flooring are a hallmark throughout the building. Hotel Mamá also has a roof terrace with a plunge pool and solarium that offers views over the old town and, to the north, the Tramuntana mountains.

Plaça de Cort, 07001 Palma
www.hotelmama.es

EAT

WITH COFFEE

LA MOLIENDA

TRENDY SPECIALTY COFFEE BAR

Run by proud Majorcan natives Miguel, Tony and Maria Jose, La Molienda is the first coffee bar where great and fair trade coffee along with delicious home cooked food and Spanish hospitality rule. The entire concept reminds of the typical Berlin-style cafes, where industrial chic offer local products. The terrace at La Molienda invites everyone to enjoy a good morning coffee for a perfect start to the day. The breakfast menu is focused on conscious eating while using local, seasonal and organically certified ingredients. The eggs, avocados, milk products and olive oils are carefully selected and sourced from small local businesses.

Carrer del Bisbe Campins, 11, 07012 Palma
www.lamolienda.es

ZIVA TO GO

NOT JUST A DIET

Ziva aims to support all humans with optimally nutritious foods while also supporting the health of the planet. The philosophy at Ziva is that food should be served in its most natural state, prepared without processed sugar, dairy, preservatives or coloring. Dishes with locally grown produce and ingredients, served in an environment that has a gourmet flare, make Ziva unique. Additionally, all containers are biodegradable and compostable. Ziva also offers a 3-step cleansing program. Together with a Ziva staff member, guests will choose the level most suitable for them to start the guided detox program.

Carrer de la Protectora, 1, 07012 Palma

www.zivatogo.com

MUSHROOM HOT
MATCHA LATTE
MATCHA TEA
ZIVA CHAI
CHAI TEA LATTE
TEA

CLARO

TRENDY IN EVERY WAY

In the heart of Palma, opposite the market Mercat de Santa Catalina, is a hot spot: Café Claro. The guest who manages to get a seat is lucky. Café Claro is always full during breakfast and lunch time. In addition to traditional Spanish snacks and dishes, one can also get Italian and international food here. With a choice of healthy muesli, chia seed pudding or classic coffee, everyone will be satisfied, including vegetarians and vegans. Café Claro is trendy in every way. The clean, bright, simple but solid decor also in combination with the food attracts many visitors as well as locals.

Calle Anibal, 16b, 07013 Palma
www.claromallorca.es

SIMPLY DELICIOUS BY RONEN

HEALTHY EASTERN MEDITERRANEAN

This vegan friendly restaurant is a melting pot of passions, fresh healthy Eastern Mediterranean cooking and above all the happiness of those who eat the dishes. Located in the Santa Catalina's neighborhood, this healthy Eastern Mediterranean restaurant serves high quality dishes, some with meat but mostly vegetarian and a few vegan dishes like a daily vegan salad. It is focused on making hummus with different toppings. The owner, Ronen Levy, began Simply Delicious with the idea that guests should feel at home as if they were eating in their living room. This eatery offers a culinary journey with flavours from Palma to native Israel.

Plaça de la Navegació, 5, 07013 Palma
www.simplydelicious.es

SANTINA BRUNCH & MORE

HEALTHY FOOD CONCEPT

Opposite to Santa Catalina's food market one will find a space of creative spirits welcoming everyone to enjoy a fruity drink or a bowl of superfoods. Situated in Palma's trendiest area, Santina offers authentic, fresh and natural products including vegan and gluten free options with a relaxed vibe. Santina's motto is clear: Making food for a city that loves to eat it. No wonder this restaurant resembles Majorcan lifestyle - smart-casual, healthy and very passionate. The dishes are prepared and presented with love.

Carrer d'Anníbal, 19, 07013 Palma
www.santinapalma.com

MAMA CARMEN'S

A TASTE OF VEGAN

Situated in the trendy area Santa-Catalina this tiny vegan gem offers a variety of yogurts, colourful and sweet fruits, variations of classic avocado toast, freshly squeezed juices, pastries and breads such as beetroot bread and turmeric rolls. Mama Carmen's caters to every taste, for vegans as well as the very conscious among us. The majority of all products are ecological and sourced from the region, There is a large marble table at the centre of this Café while there are also bar stools and the possibility of sitting on the square outside the Café.

Carrer de Cervantes, 21, 07013 Palma
www.mamacarmen.es

.9
2.5
2.1
2.4
1.7
2.7
2.6
3.0
2.3

e filtro

* 60 (1/2 per) **
Chemex (3/6 per) ** 3.5/6.0
Aeropress ** 4.3/9.0
Batch brew 4.0
Cold Brew 2.7
.... 3.5

Cafes especiales

Latte macchiato ....
Pumpking spice latte 4.8
Capuccino picante 3.8
Doble espresso con suao 3.5
Dirty chai (single espresso) 4.5
Dirty chocolate (single espresso) . 4.5

Cafes frios

Ice latte (doble shot) ....
Ice latte small (doble shot) 5.5
Frappe (doble shot) 4.5
Frappe latte (doble shot) 3.5
Frappe latte large (doble shot) ... 5.0
Espresso tonic (doble shot) 6.0
Cold Brew con leche 5.5
Batch brew ice latte 4.5
Extra - leches vegetales Bio 5.0
.... 0.5

**De 10am a 12:30

PALMA SPORT & TENNIS CLUB

THOROUGHLY HEALTHY

Palma Sport & Tennis Club is a place of diversity. In addition to 5 first-class tennis courts, a beautiful landscaped outdoor swimming pool, a fitness centre (fully stocked with the latest gear and training equipment), a yoga and Pilates centre as well as a climbing wall are available here. The tennis club takes a holistic approach towards the body, mind and enjoyment of foods. The entire facility was redeveloped by the owners, a Swedish couple Mikael and Johanna Landström. On 10,000 square meters, Palma Sport & Tennis Club provides a green oasis in the city centre for everyone and for an all-round pampering experience – or just a great lunch in a sporty environment.

Joan Maria Thomás 4, 07014 Palma
www.palmatennis.com

LA MÉMÉ

COSMOPOLITAN FEELING

Among a large number of available restaurants, sometimes it can be hard to choose. A useful mantra can be "eat where the locals eat" and La Mémé fits that phrase perfectly. From lawyers to chicas and chicos to young and older couples to visitors to politicians - this quality-conscious restaurant, serving Spanish cuisine in a stylish interior and a vintage décor, has something to offer for everyone. The daily-changing three-course lunch menu offers a choice of four starters, four mains, and eight home-made desserts. There's also an à la carte menu, offering starters, rice and pasta dishes, salads, vegetarian, meat, and fish dishes. Although not directly in Palmas city centre, La Mémé is still conveniently situated on the Avinguda del Comte de Sallent.

Avenida del Comte de Sallent, 14, 07003 Palma
www.restaurantelameme.com

EAT

WITH WINE

TOQUE DE QUEDA

BUZZING MIXTURE OF BAR AND RESTAURANT

A small window in one of Palma's narrow streets shines a brighter than others. Looking through this window confirms that eating here will lead to a busy and fun night. Once an old Bakery, now a popular restaurant giving a feeling of being in a family kitchen. Toque de Queda is a buzzing mixture of bar and restaurant, with a long, shared table in the main room, and some smaller niches. The tapas selection is generous: from Sushi de Quesos via Patatas al Horno to Zucchini Carpaccio. Toque de Queda is a hot spot to meet for a drink with friends as well as a great place for a quick snack or a long dinner.

Carrer de Can Cavalleria, 15B, 07012 Palma
no website

LA ROSA CHICA

HOT SPOT VERMUTERÍA

"The Chica" is the place to be for Majorcans and island connoisseurs. Always jam-packed, this is the right place to begin the evening in Palma with Tapas, vino or vermouth. Chic tables and chairs in front white tiled walls are a delight for all visitors. One can also sit under dried peppers, garlic and ham hanging from the ceiling. A stylish Martini advertising board and the well-known fish preserves with sardines and co. in the display complete the retro charm of this Bodega.

Carrer de Monsenyor Palmer, 5, 07014 Palma
no website

SPOT

COZY, BUT STYLISH MEDITERRANEAN

Spot is a truly Mediterranean meeting place with a commitment to local products, both in the kitchen and in its design. It features a cosy, stylish Mediterranean atmosphere during all timex of the day, whether for sipping a cocktail, getting a coffee or piece of home-made cake or having lunch and dinner with friends. Spot's menu is split into the following sections: to share, pastas, greens, soups and salads, pizza (from wood-fired oven), and from the world. The interior is covered in Mediterranean colours through wooden walls and terracotta. The décor with tiles and ceramics from the island reflect Mallorca. Large windows offer a view into the courtyard with a couple of citrus trees.

Plaça de la Verge del Miracle, 3, 07013 Palma
www.encompaniadelobos.com/spot-mallorca

AMAYA

NEW WORLD CUISINE

While modern, Amaya is a restaurant with a classic touch in Santa Catalina. An antique stone floor, a ceiling lined with more than two hundred original Majorcan window shutters, dark green tiles from Morocco and décor with authentic, high-quality furnishings give the restaurant an urban twist. As for the menu, the Mediterranean is the main source of inspiration combined with traditional recipes and delicacies from all over the world. One has to be open and curious here to discover unique tastes and unknown nuances. All dishes consist mainly of fresh, seasonal produce from local markets. Everything on the menu is homemade and freshly prepared from scratch every day.

Carrer de la Fàbrica, 18, 07013 Palma
www.amaya.one

DUKE

SURFBOARDS & MODERN DINING

Duke is one of the well known restaurants in Santa Catalina. It's a surfer's paradise offering good food in a relaxed atmosphere. The products are sourced from local farmers; the meats from butchers who care; the fish is sustainably fished in the Mediterranean and the wines are sourced from the finest bodegas in Spain. The interior reflects the surfer lifestyle of the owners, Juanjo and Ronny. Posters of VW buses, longboards and pictures of huge waves on the walls, earthy shades and cosy wooden tables. Duke has the charm of a beach hut and invites everyone to have a great time while being kind to mother earth.

Carrer Soler, 36, 07013 Palma
www.dukepalma.com

EMILIO INNOBAR

CULINARY MASTERMIND

Emilio is well known in Palma and those who have had the chance to indulge in the star chef's culinary delicacies will follow wherever Emilio goes. Emilio fans love the subtle blends of Mexican, Asian and Mediterranean elements, which the maestro calls "Fine Fusion". Influenced by his travels and work experiences, Emilio offers fresh produce every day. Emilio is one of the most popular places to visit on weekends. Hence a reservation is necessary if one wants to sit at the coveted table with a view of the kitchen and watch Emilio filleting wafer-thin fish with sinfully expensive Japan knives.

Carrer de la Concepció, 9, 07012 Palma
www.emilioinnobar.com

CANELA

MEDITERRANEAN-ASIAN FUSION

This charming restaurant, off Jaime III in the heart of Palma de Mallorca, is a gem in a narrow street. One has to look carefully to find the door. This small restaurant, which opened in 2013, has blossomed to one of the trendiest addresses in the Majorcan city. A reservation for a table is necessary, especially on weekends. The local owner and chef Fabian Fuster and his partner Irene Rigo offer an exquisite restaurant where customers can watch the kitchen team creating and plating international cuisine with a hint of Asia and an affectionate local twist.

Carrer Sant Jaume, 13, 07012 Palma
www.canelapalma.com

BAR ESPAÑA

MOST POPULAR TAPAS BAR

Situated close to Placa Mallorca in the city centre, this rustic bar is not only famous for its good selection of wines, beers and tapas, but is also a legend within the Majorcan scene and the personification of the Spanish feeling. Bar España gets full quickly after 10pm as the locals get ready for the fiesta de la noche to dance into the evening. When it comes to food, freshly baked Tortilla de Patatas, which are presented on the bar counter with other Spanish snacks, are popular among the visitors.

Carrer de Can Escursac, 12, 07001 Palma
www.facebook.com/barespanyapalma/info

TAST CLUB

ELEGANT, WARM AND INTIMATE

This club in the heart of Palma is a pearl that should not be missed. The adventure begins with the quest to find the club in the narrow romantic streets of the old part of the town. Once found, Tast Club, reminiscent of old stylish English clubs, welcomes one and all to an elegant, warm and intimate environment where typical Majorcan tapas like croquetas, pan de cristal or tomato salad are served. The thirsty can savour beautifully crafted cocktails. The interior is raw and decadent with cooling brick walls and voluptuous chandeliers. The Tast Club, spacious and yet intimate, is a great place for special occasions and a classy, adult night out.

Carrer de Sant Jaume, 6, 07012 Palma
www.tast.com/es/restaurant/tast-club

VANDAL

CREATIVE FINE-DINING

Pink cotton candy with popcorn for dessert? Why not. Creative and executive chef Bernabé Caravotta is the man behind Vandal and he proposes to bring the best of flavours, spices and ingredients from all over the world together. Popular dishes include the Japanese-Peruvian marinated eel with foie gras and shisho, the Black Angus Asado, the Spanish-Thai Langoustines with Thai sauce which is tantalizing and pair-able with the dessert called, "memories of my childhood" - cotton candy and popcorn. The drinks on offer are a speciality of Vandal as individual mini-cocktails have been created for ten dishes on the menu.

Plaça del Progrés, 15, 07013 Palma
www.vandalpalma.com

BUSCANDO EL NORTE

MODERN-MEDITERRANEAN CUISINE

This authentic Spanish restaurant is very popular, especially among locals. During the day, Buscando El Norte offers tapas and light lunch. In the evening, lobster, sharing dishes of tuna tataki with guacamole, and salad on a yellow garlic sauce are popular. Majoran wines and cocktails support the easy-going atmosphere. The cuisine is modern Mediterranean with Galician influences.

Eating at Buscando el Norte is more than just an evening out. This restaurant is about an evening out in Palma, where one gets into their best clothes and wears red lipstick. The place provides an incomparable environment, where every detail is taken care of.

Carrer de Sant Miquel, 77, 07002 Palma
www.restaurantebuscandoelnorte.com

PATRON LUNARES

TRIBUTE TO A FISHER LEGEND

This trendy restaurant, located in Mallorca's Santa Catalina neighbourhood, owes its name to a Majorcan captain. Patron Lunares was a real man, a simple and charismatic fisherman who has gone down in history not only for being one of the best bosses of his time, but also for representing the love for work, social awareness and promoting cooperation between neighbours. Today, this restaurant gives the same importance to local fish as to those from far away. Respecting the gods of the seas and mother earth, Patron Lunares uses organic meats and vegetables from Mallorca.

Carrer de la Fàbrica, 30, 07013 Palma
www.patronlunares.com

BALAGAN BY ETOH

FUNKY MIDDLE EAST TO SHARE

Balagan is a Hebrew word meaning something like "organized chaos". Here, one believes that only funkiness brings people together. This restaurant offers plates to share; it is a place to laugh and to enjoy every moment with friends, family and even strangers. Middle-Eastern and Mediterranean dishes, with meat, fish as well as vegetarian options are the focus of this restaurant, which is located in Palma's Santa Catalina district. Basic dishes such as hummus or falafel, mussels or lamb kebab are heartily seasoned and served with many new ingredients or side dishes. Owner Bogdan Tataru says that the social concept of Balagan is "food sharing", and hence the subtitle of the restaurant - "swinger-food".

Carrer d'Anníbal, 12A, 07013 Palma
www.balaganbyetoh.com

CLANDESTÍ TALLER GASTRONÒMIC

A CELEBRATION OF FOOD

A hidden place. A secret menu. Strangers at a table. Clandestí Taller Gastronòmic offers sociable gastronomic events with Majorcan culinary experience. A maximum of 16 people share an intimate experience, watching the chefs in action behind the counter. Working exclusively on reservations, the couple, Pau and Ariadna, shop at local markets and cook daily for the guests with reservation. All guests eat lunch or dinner together in a stylish contemporary setting. The menu, however, is a surprise. What is known before-hand is that all meals start with an assortment of finger food and end with Ariadna's delicious petits fours, while every dish is paired with music.

Carrer de Guillem Massot, 45, 07003 Palma
www.clandesti.es

ROSA DEL MAR

NEWEST ADDITION TO FINE-DINING

Freshly caught fish can be indulged close to Palma's port at the restaurant Rosa del Mar, one of the newest fine dining additions in the city. It is a quiet and dignified place; not a restaurant for a quick snack. In fact, Rosa del Mar impersonates the passion and emotion of Spain, the never-in-a-hurry relaxedness and the joy of life. The restaurant offers delicious and high quality Spanish food - Majorcan and Iberian - such as lobster and fried eggs with a Majorcan essence. The wine list at Rosa del Mal deserves a mention as it includes almost hundred references and signature wines from the island made with local grapes.

Darsena Ca'n Barbara, 07015 Palma
www.rosadelmarrestaurante.com

LA PARADA DEL MAR

FINEST, FRESH FISH

It can't get fresher than at La Parada del Mar - a fish and seafood restaurant with the best value for money. When entering the restaurant, the first thing to notice is a fish market. All the food that ends up on the plate later can be chosen here. Every kind of seafood is available, from fresh fish to squid, prawns, razor clams, scallops, oysters, mussels and lobsters, as well as salads. There is also a tasting menu with eight courses. The restaurant's fishing-themed dining room makes eating out here an experience with real ocean vibes.

Avinguda de Joan Miró, 244, 07015 Palma
www.laparadadelmar.com

EL BUNGALOW

LUBINA A LA SAL

Is it possible to feel, see and taste Mallorca in one day at one location? Yes! The whitewashed restaurant El Bungalow in the area Ciudad Jardin, a popular among locals at the weekend, is the place to be. Sandy feet and salty kisses, great Majorcan wines and fresh seafood such as mussels, chipirones, boquerones enjoyed during romantic sunsets make this a place to spend quality time. Built in the 1920s as a holiday home, El Bungalow has retained its original charm. Overlooking the cathedral and the cityscape of Palma de Mallorca, this must-visit restaurant to eat fresh fish or great paella has been an institution for years, making it necessary to reserve a table in advance.

Carrer d'Esculls, 2, 07007 Palma
www.rtebungalow.com

DRINK

GINBO

GIN SPECIALIST

Ginbo is a Gin Palace serving high quality gins from all over the world, including the products of Mallorca. More than 120 gin varieties and flavours combined with knowledgeable bar keepers make Ginbo extremely popular. Ginbo's magicians , with friendly smiles, behind the bar mix each drink with care and artistry. As each gin has different flavours and botanicals, each one is prepared differently and served with different fruits to best compliment the flavours. In the afternoon, this bar is a good place for a post-shopping cooling gin and tonic. In the evening, Ginbo turns into a lounge bar with moody light shining through hundreds of bottles at the bar.

Passeig de Mallorca, 14A, 07012 Palma
www.facebook.com/GINBOPalma

EL AQUANAUTA

PACIFIC FLARE FOR HAPPY PEOPLE

At the end of Avinguda de l'Argentina lies El Aquanauta, a bar and restaurant that brings Pacific flair to Palma and is extremely popular among locals. With an authentic Mexican-Californian twist, El Aquanauta serves tacos and tropical drinks in a surf-inspired atmosphere. The colours of the walls reflect the sunset in the ocean and surfer pictures on the wall inspires visitors to grab a board and ride some waves. The cosy restaurant consists of several rooms, each with only two or three tables. Different types of tacos, quesadillas, nachos, margaritas, tostadas, guacamole and lots of gluten-free and vegetarian dishes are on the menu. Fish, ceviche or pulpo are popular at this colourful restaurant.

Avinguda de l'Argentina, 27, 07013 Palma
www.elaquanauta.com

ROXY BEACH

CHILL-OUT BEACH SPOT

This beach bar is an institution for many locals and regular visitors to Mallorca. Situated at the end of the beach in Portal Nous, Roxy Beach Bar is accessible via the steps from Portals Nous town. Strawberry Daiquiris, Mojitos, Vinos or Espresso on the rocks can be enjoyed with a magnificent view of the sea and a pleasant midsummer breeze. Jet Ski riders might pass by. However, the beach-front remains calm and the water crystal clear. Watching the sunset is extremely popular here and in the evening DJs play loungey tunes to the rhythm of the waves.

Carrer d'en Blanes, 10, 07181 Portals Nous
no website

UM THE BEACH HOUSE

ELEGANT BOHO STYLE

Imagine living in a beach house located alongside crystal clear waters. That dream can come true with the UM Beach House Concept. The first Umami beach house is located in Portal Nous/Illetas, one of the highly esteemed areas of Mallorca. An exquisite atmosphere can be enjoyed at the marina, at the beach and in the city, as Palma is not far. At this beach house, summer becomes a lifestyle, and the boho style represents the Majorcan landscape in an elegant way. Experience a true Majorcan touch in relaxed and elegant Mediterranean surroundings.

Positivity, humanity, warmth, know-how and of course passion are the values which will transform each visitor when staying in this unique beach house on the Spanish Island.

Ctra Palma-Andratx km11, Costa D'en Blanes, Calvia 07181
www.umthebeachhouse.com

EL GARITO

THE CLUB TO BE SEEN AT

El Garito is probably the most popular bar of Palma's nightlife. Though tiny in size, the popularity of El Garito attracts everyone to the bar, no matter how full it is. Numerous art exhibitions have been held here and the work of many local artists are hung on the walls. In the afternoon, El Garito is a café while it turns into a bar and club in the evening. The protagonist: music. From fusion jazz and pure jazz to electronic music; the vibe remains relaxed and loungy.

Dársena de Can Barbara, s/n, 07015 Palma de Mallorca
www.garitocafe.com

VENTUNO BAR

ITALIAN NIGHT OUT

Away from the buzzing tourist hot spot, this little bar offers Italian dolce vita in Palma de Mallorca. The big wine glass on the house wall invites everyone to unwind and relax. The Ventuno Bar, barely bigger than a table tennis table, is a well-kept secret which is always lively and filled with people drinking Aperol Spritz or Negroni. It cannot get better than starting the night at an Italian bar into a Majorcan Fiesta de la noche with Italian-inspired tapas or mini pizzas. And if there is no seat or table available, enjoy the music and a table will be available in a couple of minutes.

Carrer de Sant Magí 60, 07013 Palma
www.ventunobar.com

SHOP

ADDICT

CAREFULLY SELECTED CLOTHES

Owned by the same duo as nearby La Principal, Addict was their first project and has been at the vanguard of Palma's fashion scene. The boutique is lit and seductive, offering well organized shelves with not too many and not too little to choose. Addict sells selected brands such as Norse Projects, Fillipa K., Veja, Le Coq Sportif, BWGH or the Majorcan brand Mews as well as offering elegant clothing from other brands. The clothes from Mews (its leather and suede goods are made on the island) are designed to be comfortable, relaxed, colourful and most importantly – real. For Majorcan shoppers, it is important that the clothes is wearable with a truly Majorcan feel, laid back, yet smart – simply Mediterranean.

Carrer de Can Danús, 4, 07001 Palma
no website

LA LIBELULA HOME

ETHICAL HOMEWARE PRODUCTS

It is not uncommon that travelers share their life on the road. The day Kate and John met was the beginning of La Libelula Home. The couple talked for 29 hours and then decided to embark on a life together in Mallorca. Today, La Libelula Home is a heaven for homeware, furniture, decoration, interior design and children's ware in the heart of Palma's Santa Catalina. The shop offers decor with a preference for sustainable brands and recycled materials. This rustic modern shop is not only full of treasures from all over the world, it is also full of love and life. Rumor has it that one will find it hard to leave La Libelula empty-handed.

Carrer de Pou 22, 07013 Palma
www.lalibelulahome.com

VIVECA

ANTIQUES & HANDMADE SHOP

Located in a backyard in a converted garage, Viveca is an interior shop with both new and antique items. From small glasses and vases to furniture like desks and bookcases, there are a wide variety of products from around the world, such as handmade wooden products and ceramics from Morocco and antique pieces from the Netherlands. Viveca offers a dose of island inspiration and interior and landscape design services. Along with other design and concept stores, Viveca shows that Mallorca now leads the way with a thriving design scene. Both, the Spanish Vogue and Architectural Digest have rated Viveca highly.

Carrer de Sant Feliu, 17, 07012 Palma
no website

BAZAAR

CREATIVE, HAND-MADE GOODS

At Bazaar Palma everything is about home and design. Situated in the old part of the town, this former bookshop sells candles, glassware, kitchenware, textiles and natural cosmetic products from L:A Bruket and MALIN + GOETZ. The floor tiles, wooden bookcases and display cabinets are still in their original condition, which makes shopping at Bazaar Palma a special experience. Finest porcelain, delicate napkins, handmade tableware as well as ceramics for fruits and unusual cutlery can be found here. This is heaven for Décor-fans, rustic with a touch of glamour. One or two items bought from Bazaar make for an ideal souvenir and memory of Mallorca.

Costa d'en Brossa, 17A, 07001 Palma
no website

BON VIVANT

WITH LOVE FOR DETAILS

This shop is for all who love details and décor. Bon Vivant offers everything from tailor-made modular sideboards to custom cabinets to energy-efficient homes to children's bedroom décor. One can even order custom-made design for home offices; the list is endless. The shop itself is bright and friendly, providing carefully curated items for all design lovers. Bon Vivant specialises in interior design and treasures from around the world. Bon Vivant not only offers a unique shopping experience, but also shows that Palma is a Mediterranean city that offers a cosmopolitan experience and exclusive shops and items.

Carrer dels Horts, 8, 07003 Palma
no website

ONE DREAM, ONE GOAL AND A TALENTED
TEAM THAT TOGETHER WITH THEIR
MENTORS CREATE INDEPENDENT MINDED
LIVING CONCEPTS.

THE DESIGN DISTRICT IS A DESTINATION
WHERE IMAGINATION, PASSION FOR
DESIGN AND CAREFULLY THOUGHT
SPACES & CONCEPTS ARE CONCEIVED FOR
THE JOY AND PLEASURE OF US ALL.
A PLACE WHERE IDEAS TAKE ACTION BY
SHARING OUR INTENTIONS TO TELL
MEANINGFUL STORIES, A TREASURE
CHEST FILLED WITH AMAZING GIFTS AND
PROJECTS FOR A BEAUTIFUL NEW WORLD.

MAKING THE ORDINARY
TRULY EXTRAORDINARY

BCONNECTED
LIVING CONCEPTS

Christine Leja
DESIGNER & VISIONARY

BCONNECTED

PASSION FOR DESIGN

Located in the heart of Santa Catalina, Bconnected Living Concepts welcomes industry professionals and discerning shoppers with neon letters and offers a unique design destination to source materials, buy something special and get inspired. A curated selection of furniture, lighting, home accessories and artwork brings a new, holistic approach to design and interiors by integrating all of the elements that go into building a home. Whether one is looking for well-crafted objects, quality materials, vibrant colors, or original designs, Palma's Design District is the place to go to. Even customized furniture, carpets or lights can be ordered here.

Calle dameto 4 - 6, Santa Catalina, 07013 Palma
www.bconnectedmallorca.com

RIALTO LIVING

THOROUGH LIFESTYLE CONCEPT

Rialto Living is housed in a 15th century building, a historic cinema palace in the old town of Palma. Founded by the Swedes, Klas Käll and Barbara Bergman, who created this 800 square meter shopping heaven where everything from fashion to furniture, books, art and accessories can be found. This beautiful luxurious store is considered by many to be the best on the island. The home décor ranges from an eclectic array of styles such as the New York Collection offering a cool, elegant and urban concept to ethnic collection conveying a natural, relaxed and rustic vibe in earthy colours. The hungry ones can enjoy fresh food and juices at the café, a former theatre stage at the back of the store.

Carrer de Sant Feliu, 3, 07012 Palma
www.rialtoliving.com

LA PRINICIPAL

KEY PLAYER IN MENSWEAR

This boutique is a key player in Palma's menswear scene and caters to stylish men who care about quality. The window-display and the immaculately stylish interior are irresistible to enter. La Principal sells a carefully selected range of clothes from brands such as Maison Kitsuné, Homecore, Riding High, Rains and the Majorcan brand Mews, as well as shoes from Spalwart, Novesta and Veja. It's a pleasure to pop around and browse through the long racks. La Principal is owned by the same duo as nearby Addict, the founders of the local brand Mews. The founders' style and passion reflects the new vibrant Palma – simply buzzing with creativity and entrepreneurship.

Carrer dels Paraires, 5, 07001 Palma
no website

EXPLORE

Relax, and breathe. Mallorca invites you to slow down, and to take a break from your daily routine. Beautiful Finca hotels and holistic retreats offer an atmosphere of quietness and recreation. In the explore category, you'll find personally selected hotels and holiday houses with style and charm on the whole island.

SON BRULL HOTEL & SPA

A LUXURIOUS RURAL SANCTUARY

At the foot of the Sierra de Tramuntana, close to beautiful beaches, the Formentor Peninsula and the quaint town of Pollensa, Son Brull Hotel & Spa is situated. Originally a Jesuit monastery from the 18th century, this 5-star hotel offers contemporary design and an impression of the authentic Mallorca. This is not only conveyed through the design, but also with the food and in the spa. Locally grown and organic products tickle your palate while the spa pampers you with natural products of Mallorca. Additionally, Son Brull is committed to renewable energy, recycling, preservation of native varieties and the unconditional support of local producers. In five words, the Son Brull Boutique Hotel & Spa is authentic, respectful, cultural, traditional and offers a rich heritage.

Ctra. Palma - Puerto Pollença, Km. 50, 07460 Pollença
www.sonbrull.com

ESPLÉNDIDO

BOUTIQUE- AND DESIGN-HOTEL

Situated at the frontline position in Port Soller, Hotel Espléndido is facing the seafront and offers two pools, a restaurant and a lush rooftop. Built in 1954, the relaxed vintage feel of the hotel is still alive with its fifties furniture, lighting and design. The wide lobby is full of natural light and casts its gaze straight across the esplanade onto the sea. Sandy beaches are just a two-minute walk from the hotel and the a 30-minutes stroll to Sa Muleta lighthouse offers spectacular views. The cozy Bistro restaurant with open kitchen on the ground floor overlooks the port's promenade and offers a diverse à la carte lunch and evening menu to suit all tastes from 1pm-11pm.

Es Traves, 5, 07100 Soller
www.esplendidohotel.com

BIKINI ISLAND & MOUNTAIN HOTELS

LUXURIOUS HIPPIE-CHIC

True to the motto "Life is better in a bikini" – with or without wearing one - this hotel offers its guests time to relax at the Port de Sóller Bay, with a view of the Tramuntana Mountains. The romantic harbor bay is a gem among Mallorca's seaside places. From the hotel nestled between the seaside village and the lemon groves, travelers can stroll along the bay, sip coffee or relax on the beach. For adventurers, the Tramuntana Mountains offer trekking and mountain biking trails. Besides the beach and the promenade, those feeling the urge to mingle with people can visit the cocktail bar Pikkini, which offers colorful drinks and homemade oriental lemonades. After all, being carefree and happy are the main tasks one has to do at Bikini.

Carrer de Migjorn, 2, 07108 Port de Sóller
www.bikini-hotels.com

PREDI SON JAUMELL

PERFECT PLACE TO UNWIND

At this hotel, nature is the most precious asset. Son Jaumell offers guests a few days of tranquility, in pure contact with nature, with all the benefits of relaxing in a rural setting. This luxury retreat is housed in a 17th-century building and surrounded by the tranquil Majorcan countryside, close to lush forestland. At Son Jaumell, everything is designed for ultimate relaxation, making it the perfect location for an escape from your daily routine. Each room has been decorated with a different unique style. From our terraces, you can enjoy the view of the imposing medieval castle of Capdepera - one of the best conserved and most charming towns on the island.

Cala Mesquida, Km 1, 07580 Capdepera
www.hotelsonjaumell.com

CAP ROCAT

TOTAL TRANQUILLITY& LUXURY

Who would have thought that a former military fortress can be transformed into an exceptional boutique hotel with two pools and restaurants and a spa? Close to rugged coastline, Cap Rocat is a heaven of peace, offering complete privacy. Situated at Cala Blava on the edge of a nature reserve, it offers panoramic views of Palma Bay. The former sandstone military fort provides a comfortable, mysterious and chic living space. With its wide subterranean labyrinthine paths and giant gates, it could be a film set mixed with ancient citadel features. Natural stone, marble, timber ceilings and mellow lighting are combined with furnishings in neutral tones. Cap Rocat has been created for a restful ambience for the body and the mind.

Ctra. d'enderrocat, s/n, 07609 Cala Blava-Llucmajor
www.caprocat.com

BOUTIQUEHOMES

HOLIDAY HOUSES FOR DESIGN LOVERS

Travelers looking to discover the world with style will feel excited about BoutiqueHomes. Here, style is more an obsession than the mere idea to decorate. All homes are intriguing and imaginative; visitors get to see the world through the eyes of the owners. Rather than flashy luxury items, the BoutiqueHomes offer soul. Dramatic locations, in which details matter, create an experience that no one will forget. The homeowners share stories of the properties, serendipitous discoveries, and that special feeling of falling in love with a place. For this reason, BoutiqueHomes set up a community exchange: reward points can be redeemed at a marketplace, a store, or shared with other creatives within the community.

www.boutique-homes.com

MONTUIRI VILLAGE

A STORY OF TRAVEL, DESIGN AND INSPIRATION

Only a five-minute walk from the main square of Montuiri, this accommodation in Mallorca offers peaceful country village living and unobstructed views of the breathtaking Tramuntana mountains. Discovered by a German stylist, this home tells a personal story: it's filled with a one-of-a-kind style and personality, situated in a charming island village full of life. The whitewashed facades draw attention to the house and the large windows let natural light flood into the oasis inside. Each corner of the house is loaded with designs inspired by traveling the world. All sorts of items from various destinations - from bull skulls to Portuguese porcelain – come together to tell their stories. The tropical lush garden offers shade and coolness in the summer heat.

booking via
www.boutique-homes.com

MALLORCA VILLA

DARING EXAMPLE OF LESS IS MORE

Less is more, and Zen is all. To be able to understand this credo, a visit to the Mallorca Villa is a must. Set in an almond grove on the southern part of the island, the architecture and the landscape melt into each other and shine all the brighter for being combined. Mallorca Villa was designed by John Pawson and Claudio Silvestrin, the duo responsible for designing leading retail locations for Calvin Klein and Giorgio Armani. This Villa manages to express emotions and feelings, it is an art installation, and its clean, sharp, delineated lines of vertical and geometric shapes evoke a modern take on antiquity. This spacious home features five bedrooms that sleep a total of eleven guests.

booking via
www.boutique-homes.com

COPYRIGHT

The publisher would like to thank the following for their kind permission to reproduce their photographs:

Es Princep p.8; Portixol p.12-17; Es Princep p.18-23; Hotel Nakar p.24-28; Hotel Sant Francesc p.30-35; Summum Hotel p.36-38; Hotel Cort p.42; Hotel Mamá p.44-47; La Molienda p.50; Palma Sport & Tennis Club p.74-77; Patron Lunares p.120; El Garito p.152; Viveca p.162; Bazaar p.164; Son Brull p.178-183; Espléndido p. 184-179; Bikini Hotel p.190-193; Predi Son Jaumell p.194-197; Cap Rocat p.198-203; Boutique Homes p.204-215